GENERATION
STARTUP

GENERATION STARTUP

Become the CEO of Your Life

innovation
publishing

ISBN-13: 978-0-578-94354-1
ISBN-10: 0-578-94354-9

Cover design by: Leah Jay
Editors: Andrew Adam, Kathy Miserendino
Printed in the United States of America

To all my dear friends and family.

"In the joy of others, lies our own."

PRAMUKH SWAMI MAHARAJ

"If someone wants to accomplish great things, there is no better place than the United States."

ELON MUSK

INTRODUCTION

My name is Ronak Patel and I am a 21- year old entrepreneur and activist. I have always loved everything about entrepreneurship and the American dream and hope to share some of my passion with you in this book. While I have a lot of room for growth as an entrepreneur and person myself, I wrote the chapters in this book to highlight some of the key things I have learned in my endeavors.

In the first chapter, I write about some of the best examples of the American dream in my life and I hope this chapter inspires you to see our country in a way so many immigrants do. In the subsequent chapters, I cover important career topics like mindset, execution, relationships, innovation, personal finance, and servant leadership. I hope these chapters lead you to further explore these subjects and take action in your life.

In the last chapter, I provide some insight on the publishing process and how something like publishing a book is within your reach. Ultimately, I hope something in this book gives you inspirations or ideas to pursue your dreams.

While Andrew Adam and Kathy Miserendino have been fantastic editors and consultants throughout this process, I am completely responsibile for any typos or stylstic errors that you may see. I wanted to get this book to market quickly and I am sure there are several errors. I hope that does not take away from the poential value of this book. Also, I want to thank Leah Jay for helping with the cover art for this book.

After the acknowledgements, there are organized pages where you are able to take notes. Happy reading and good luck!

CONTENTS

CHAPTER 1: THE AMERICAN DREAM

Ever since I was a kid, I have been in awe of the United States and everything our country offers. Like many of my first-generation American peers, my parents came to this country for the immense economic opportunities and freedoms. According to a 2020 Pew Research Center article, more than 40 million people living in the U.S. were born in another country, accounting for about one-fifth of the world's migrants.

Unfortunately, many people in my generation seem to have lost faith in the American dream or even believe that it never existed in the first place. I wholeheartedly believe that the American dream is alive and better than ever.

Our politicians and public figures use talking points and soundbites surrounding this concept. However, the American Dream is not a talking point or soundbite for me; It is my life story. I grew up witnessing the American dream firsthand almost every second of my life. I am a proud son of two immigrant parents from India who continue to remind me of what this country offers each day.

When my parents arrived in this country, they came with almost nothing. They did not come here with an education or a significant sum of money. They barely spoke English and had to start working immediately to cover their living expenses. After getting married in the United States, they worked up to 14 hours a day at Dunkin Donuts, selling coffee and donuts to customers in the northern New Jersey area.

They started off working minimum wage jobs but were already grateful for that opportunity to come to work every day and earn income. My parents showcased incredible work ethic and later became managers of their respective Dunkin Donuts locations. They did not come to this country with any knowledge of managing or running a small business and were entirely outside of their comfort zone. However, their winning trait was that they did not take any opportunity for granted. Their gratitude and ambition kept them going.

A few years later, the had saved up enough money to purchase their first Subway restaurant in New Jersey. They achieved an impressive milestone and had a lot to be grateful for at this point. Buying a franchise business was their first taste of their American dream. Unfortunately, their first business did not meet performance expectations, and they ended up selling the company a few years later. Still pursuing the great American dream, they packed their bags with my brother and I, and we moved to Pennsylvania, where my parents found and acquired another Subway location.

Today, my parents own multiple businesses in the food and beverage space through constant ups and downs and are determined to keep growing their ventures. Seeing my parents start from nothing and build their businesses and wealth through countless obstacles has been nothing short of astonishing.

When I was in elementary school, my parents studied to take their U.S. citizenship exam to become naturalized citizens. They studied hard and practiced subjects like civics, English, and interview skills. I distinctly remember coming home from school the day they had their exam and interview. They were both dressed up in newly bought suits with smiles on their faces. They eventually delivered the news that they had passed their citizenship exam and scheduled their oath of allegiance ceremony.

They had finally become American citizens after a lengthy and demanding process. They had a profound feeling about being fully naturalized Americans. In recent years, they have even practiced their right to vote for our elected officials. Even though they are immigrants, they truly understand and have a unique perspective on what it means to be an American. They know all of the opportunities this country offers and the freedoms and liberties our government is supposed to protect.

With this constant reminder of the American dream in my house, I, too, wanted to take advantage of all the things this great country has to offer. Although I was eternally grateful for all the sacrifices and hard work my parents had put in, I wanted to paint my own destiny.

I experimented with many entrepreneurial ideas in high school and college. Eventually, I found the best success with my web design company, Patel Digital LLC. While people may still think it requires a lot of money or resources to start a company, it is simply not true. In addition to living in a country that allows us to pursue any idea or opportunity we think of, we also live in a digital age that opens us to a new realm of possibilities.

Indeed, some industries like healthcare and finance require significant amounts of capital to start companies. But you can create your first business or side hustle with the resources that you already have. I started my digital consulting business, which initially specialized in social media consulting, without outside investment or resources.

Although an extreme example, I acquired my first consulting client before spending a single penny. I acquired this client through LinkedIn after being connected through a classmate, so there was no client acquisition or marketing cost.

Furthermore, I had not yet invested in any resources to form a business entity, like an LLC, at this point. There is no need to create a legal entity to test out an idea. I did not even have a website or business email. I had an idea and the drive to test the market. There is no better way to receive validation on your potential business idea than testing the market.

The day before my pitch in front of the CEO and other key executives, I realized that I did not even have business cards. So, I approached a business teacher at my high school and asked if she had cardstock paper that I could use. Luckily, she did, and she gave me a sheet.

Next, I went on one of the computers in my high school library and created a business card design on a Microsoft Word template. Funny enough, I hand cut these business cards so I ccould pass out my contact information to everyone at the pitch the next day.

After I landed the deal, I then invested those funds into a legal entity, a website, and professionally printed business cards. This lean methodology did not stop once I landed more clients. I have not spent any funds on marketing and do not invest in things that are not essential to the operation or growth of my company. Fortunately, I have been able to have a taste of the American dream early on in my life.

Regardless of being first-generation or fifth-generation, anyone can achieve their American dream. Through running Patel Digital LLC, I have met with quite a few extraordinary entrepreneurs that are outstanding examples of the American dream and what our country has to offer. One of these individuals is an attorney and activist named Dan Backer.

Dan Backer was born in the Soviet Union and came to this country when he was a kid. Knowing that his family immigrated to the United States to escape communism, he grew up with a similar admiration for our country as I did. Dan graduated law school and eventually chose to start a law firm in D.C. in the area of political law. Through his practice and activism, he has been able to affect the American political system significantly.

Dan Backer was the plaintiff's counsel in the supreme court case FEC v. McCutcheon, where they successfully eliminated aggregate donor limits. In addition, he was the plaintiff's counsel in the case FEC v. Carey, which created a new type of political action commiteee called the hybrid PAC. Dan is a leader in his area of practice and continues to protect the American dream every day, all as a naturalized American.

Because of my interest in preserving the American dream, I joined a political action committee called Maverick PAC. I have the pleasure to serve on its national membership committee. Maverick PAC contributes to congressional and senate candidates that advocate for free enterprise and limited government.

Through the Maverick PAC network, I was able to connect with an extraordinary individual named Audrey Henson. Recently, Audrey was listed on Forbes 30 under 30, but her journey is even more admirable. Growing up to a single mother in a low-income household, Audrey had many challenges.

Through hard work and determination, she landed an internship on Capitol Hill, a dream of many college aged students across the country. When she got to our nation's capital, she quickly realized she could not relate to most representatives or interns. One day, Audrey's colleagues discussed a bill relating to food stamps, and someone had made a joke about why it even mattered if recipients got a hot or cold meal.

Unlike the people laughing about this, Audrey knew the importance of these government programs because she had to rely on them. Realizing there was an apparent issue in the representation of our country, she set out to make a change. In 2016, she founded College to Congress to help secure congressional internships from diverse backgrounds throughout the country and even helping them with the financial aid to live and work in Washington, D.C.

Audrey has already made an enormous impact advocating for this cause. Traditionally, many house internships were unpaid, leaving an extreme financial burden on those without advantaged backgrounds. Audrey successfully supported creating the House Internship Fund of $48 million to go directly to paying interns.

In addition, her organization now has six people, and they had their highest intern class of twenty students in 2019. College to Congress has partnerships with more than 70 congressional offices of both parties to support their mission of increasing opportunity in public service.

Audrey and her team continue to fight for more diverse representation in our nation's capital. During the COVID-19 pandemic, they pivoted to online training by creating the College to Congress University, a platform where students are trained on how to secure internships on Capitol Hill. They are given the opportunity to partner with a mentor and apply for financial aid if they successfully secure an internship. Approximately 800 students took advantage of this online training, significantly increasing the impact and reach of College to Congress.

My parents, Dan Backer and Audrey Henson, all have a   strong desire to protect and strengthen the American dream. Regardless of their disadvantaged backgrounds and obstacles, they were able to accomplish incredible goals.

What does the American dream mean to you?

CHAPTER 2: REDEFINING SUCCESS

Success looks different for everyone. People need to start approach success with that mindset. It is easy to look at a successful entrepreneur, athlete, or artist and say they are successful, but you must define what that means for you. Everyone's true goal of success is different. Overall, I think success is achieving a lifestyle that allows you to do what you want and spend your time the way you want.

This definition of success is broad, and rightfully so, because we all have different versions of the lifestyle we want to work towards. The work and life schedule of a full-time entrepreneur and business owner will be quite different from that of a person who makes an average salary and works traditional work hours. We have different priorities, yet many of us find ourselves comparing ourselves to others, which defeats the purpose of achieving our own success or happiness.

It is undoubtedly true that financial freedom

is essential, and you need money to sustain a comfortable lifestyle for you and your family. After that level of income is reached, however, it is more important to evaluate your priorities and figure out what lifestyle you want. It is not clear which person is more successful solely based on their income. Someone that brings in a $50,000 salary can be equally or even more successful as someone that brings in millions of dollars.

If you want to join a softball team, be there for all your children's events, and spend time volunteering in your faith-based organization, then that is what your unique definition of success is. Being able to do all the things you want to do will lead you to a happy and successful life.

If you want to achieve all these things but start living a lifestyle that never allows you to do any of the things you want, are you achieving success? Or are you making life decisions based on what you think society expects of you?

Achieving entrepreneurial or business success is challenging and demanding. This book is certainly not meant to discourage entrepreneurship and innovation but instead encourage people to figure out what their goals genuinely are so they can decide their next journey or path. Running a business requires a great deal of time and energy to achieve the goal that you want to achieve. If you are not doing what aligns with your purpose, it only makes it harder for you. Also, you will not be happy with your work, and ultimately that is more important than anything else.

I want to be an entrepreneur because I have always enjoyed executing new ideas and embracing risk. I enjoy being my boss and am willing to work on my ventures every day. I do not need a vacation from my lifestyle because I am doing what I enjoy reagardless of the obstacles along the way. Many people cannot say the same because they are not doing what they genuinely love.

Additionally, there are even different goals within entrepreneurship. Starting a side hustle or a business does not mean the same to everyone. Some people might want to start a business that allows them to be their boss, but they might not want to build a million-dollar company. A part-time business owner lifestyle is probably very successful for a lot of people. They can be their boss while making the time for the things they enjoy without focusing solely on business growth.

While social media has led to unique business opportunities and the opportunity to have unprecedented levels of connections with people, we find that it is easy to compare ourselves to others and achieve their success level without understanding what their lives are truly like.

Social media is not a representation of an individual or influencer's whole life; it highlights the best parts people wish to show and use for their brand or image. People might view me as having a successful web design company after they see our client projects or influential figures on my social media feeds. Still, they are not seeing the hours I am putting in or the personal and professional struggles of being an entrepreneur.

Hence, it benefits you if you did not compare your lifestyle with an individual or influencer's posts because that is not an actual representation of their lives. You are only setting yourself up for failure if you do this.

Similarly, you should not compare your life's timeline with what you see on social media or what you think society expects from you. One of the most prominent issues I see with societal perception is that people expect to achieve certain milestones at certain times. People think they are somehow not successful if they do not fulfill these milestones or by a specific age. This mindset is only detrimental and we need to acknowledge that we will all tackle different obstacles and timelines.

What does a successful life look like for you?

CHAPTER 3:
EXECUTING IDEAS

Many college peers and high school students that I have conversations with are interested in starting a business or side hustle but do not know where to start. Because entrepreneurship is more in the public eye than ever before, many students and young adults think they want to own their own business. I am always eager and excited to hear from young people with entrepreneurial aspirations. However, sometimes expectations may be misguided and unrealistic.

It can be easy to equate entrepreneurial success with money and other lifestyle traits. While profit is a measure of business and entrepreneurial success, people are more likely to fail if they are solely chasing the financial rewards. If you define success as your freedom to do what you want, you should be figuring out how to turn your passion into your purpose.

Ever since elementary school, I had an aptitude for digital technology. I was constantly trying to test the capabilities of the newly released iPod

Touch, and many of my friends would even pay me to perform services for them. By the time I reached middle school, teachers recognized my technology savviness and even asked me to help solve technological problems. At this point, I knew I enjoyed helping people with digital issues. Still, I had no idea that I would later start a digital ser that would add value to companies and organizations around the country.

I am likely not the only one to have been passionate about certain things from a young age. In addition to technology, I was also highly interested in healthcare, business, and politics. To this day, I continue to explore these interests and take advantages of opportunities in these fields.

If you already have a starting point for what you are passionate about or skilled at, you are not too far away from a legitimate income-producing business or side hustle. In high school, I developed a keen interest in entrepreneurship, investing, and financial freedom. I found myself watching, reading, and listening to content from prolific entrepreneurs and investors. I spent a lot of time getting inspired and learning about all the possibilities when starting your own business and charting your destiny.

Like many of the same students and young adults I talk to today, I did not know where to begin. I knew I wanted to own a business and be an entrepreneur, but I had no clue where to start. As I continued absorbing content relating to entrepreneurship, I realized that social media could provide an excellent opportunity for an entrepreneurial endeavor.

The summer between my sophomore and junior year of high school, I invested my birthday money in a course taught by a very skilled marketer on Instagram and aimed to teach strategies to grow Instagram pages. I created an Instagram page with motivational content and used these strategies to attempt to grow and monetize my page. While I had amassed a few thousand followers for the page, and successfully landed a few posts on the explore page that attracted a lot of engagement, I did not find the success I wanted to with this endeavor. I ultimately was not able to monetize this page itself.

Because of this content Instagram page had created, I connected with an individual with over a million followers on Instagram, and eventually landed an income-producing opportunity with him. I was experimenting with the social media marketing world before Instagram Ads existed. Leaders in the social media marketing space predicted Instagram to follow Facebook in introducing advertising tools, but it had not happened yet. Since this individual needed help monetizing his page with over a million followers, I enthusiastically took this opportunity.

There were plenty of small business accounts, with marketing budgets, that would greatly benefit from having their product or service featured on a page with over a million followers. I was going to be the one to introduce these businesses to this marketing opportunit and receive a commission on the advertising revenue brought to the influencers' page. I also discovered my passion for networking during this time. I enjoyed talking to new business owners and listening to areas of improvement for thier businesses. I was directly messaging as many business accounts as I could see and presented them with this business opportunity to post an advertisement on this influencer's Instagram page.

I successfully brought in advertising revenue from clients across the world, including the United States, Canada, Australia, and Europe. Though I was only sixteen years of age, no one I spoke with was aware of my age because I used a business Instagram account specifically for this purpose. I made hundreds of dollars through PayPal; simply by messaging clients from my phone and presenting them with an opportunity. Eventually, Instagram would come out with cheaper Instagram advertising tools directly from their platform, and it would soon be the end of this endeavor.

This little endeavor was my first taste of entrepreneurial success in high school, and I learned key things that are still applicable to the ventures I will continue to run and start. First, you do not need to spend money on an expensive course. As I mentioned, I had used birthday money from my parents to purchase an Instagram marketing course. While the material in this course was valuable and eventually led to profitable opportunities, I did not have to make that investment. I learned that many, if not all, of the things taught and mentioned in this paid course were readily available on the internet for free or little cost. We are fortunate to live in a time that allows us to learn almost everything through text, audio, video, and even virtual reality. If you want to know about a subject or general business practices, all the resources are literally at your fingertips. If you put in the time and have an intrinsic motivation to learn about the subject, you will come to understand it.

Second, I learned how to spot an opportunity and create business value. Ultimately, people pay to have problems solved for them. That is what business is. Business is simply an exchange of value, usually currency, for a product or service that solves a problem or need for them. Profitable business opportunities can be found by looking for gaps in the market, meaning that a business problem needs to be solved. Then, you are going to make money by offering a product or service that solves this problem.

In this example, the problem was two-sided. Small businesses needed to capitalize on Instagram marketing to boost their business. On the other hand, the influencer was missing out on the opportunity to monetize his page and did not have the time. So, I came in and essentially acted as a broker between the two parties, the business owners, and the influencers, making money from allowing these business deals to occur and adding value to each other. You certainly do not need to invent a new product or service to create business value. Sometimes, it can be as simple as brokering a deal between two parties in an area you know.

Third, I learned that initial business or organization ideas seldom work out as originally intended. Therefore, pivoting should be embraced and is a common attribute among many startups. When you first launch your business idea or side hustle, do not worry about getting everything perfect. Most entrepreneurs will tell you that they go through continuous innovation. Their current business is quite different from the one they intended to start. Adapting is healthy because change is the only thing that remains constant, and your business and you need to adapt to the obstacles and innovation going on around you.

As previously mentioned, this first taste of entrepreneurial success, during high school, ended once Instagram rolled out its advertising services. After I submitted college applications, during my senior year of high school, I was eager to embark on another entrepreneurial venture. This time, I decided to leverage my only actual business knowledge, social media marketing, and launch a social media marketing agency. I was able to get my first social media consulting client in March of my senior year, before I even graduated from high school. I added value to this established manufacturing company because their marketing team was not well versed in many of the nuances of modern digital marketing. I was able to give them that perspective and teach them to solve various business problems. In the process, I learned a tremendous amount, not just about digital marketing but also other areas of business such as business development, product development, teamwork, communication, and even business law.

I was making better money with my social media consulting work than I would have at many of the jobs my peers were working. However, I still was not achieving the lifestyle I wanted, or the amount of client work I hoped to achieve, so I kept my eyes open for other opportunities. I kept reading and listening to content related to entrepreneurship. Towards the end of my senior year of high school, e-commerce and drop shipping became popular among the entrepreneurial community. I knew I wanted to give it a shot.

The week after high school graduation, my peers were out celebrating at the beach; to commemorate the ending of an important chapter in our lives. While this was happening, I was essentially creating a plan of how I would roll out an e-commerce store as soon as I could. After a few weeks, I partnered with a talented friend in design, and we launched an e-commerce store, targeted towards Generation Z, that sold merchandise such as clothing, bathing suits, and bracelets. We used organic social media reach to successfully generate sales for our e-commerce store. We tried paid advertising with a limited budget but were not able to convert any leads. With this project, I rekindled my passion for sales and was honestly impressed with what we were about to achieve. While this was a profitable venture, we did not find it to be scalable or sustainable. We re-evaluated and decided to stop working on this venture.

This e-commerce store venture also provided a lot of entrepreneurial lesson that I talk about to this day. First, I learned the economic concept of barriers to entry. We were selling products that people could find anywhere and did not have the type of differentiation or solve a specific problem that consumers had.

Second, you need to determine whether the market needs your product or service when coming out with a product or service. Sales will be the best indicator of this. To test your product or service, you need to come out with a minimum viable product or service, a product or service you can go to market with and get feedback on it.

Third, I realized again that it might lead to another idea or opportunity that you did not initially anticipate when you pursue a venture. I did not have a winning product or brand necessary to develop a successful e-commerce store. However, I learned how to design, manage, and fix problems relating to e-commerce stores. With this knowledge and experience, I could solve problems for so many businesses. Many business owners in every market and demographic have a reputable brand but flaws in their e-commerce strategy due to time or knowledge constraints. I, as an entrepreneur, could fix this problem

As my partner and I continued to run our e-commerce store, I set up a meeting with a local entrepreneur with impressive branding and marketing. We started talking about how I could add value for him, and he became incredibly interested in our e-commerce store. I offered to design an automated dropshipping e-commerce store for his brand and received $1,000 for it. This person was one of my first web design clients and the birth of the successful web design business I have been running for three years now.

As a result of my success with this first web design client, I started setting up meetings with other local business owners; pitching my web design services. I have been running for three years now. I started receiving more and more clients and I continued experimenting with this business for the past few years and have developed it into what it is today. There are certainly ups and downs in terms of revenue, due to college and other commitments. Still, overall, I have grown my web design company into a secure business that allows me to earn a lucrative income at my discretion.

Today, Patel Digital LLC has business and political clients around the entire country, has allowed me to travel worldwide, and allowed me to live the kind of lifestyle I desire as a business owner. Of course, none of this happened overnight; it took a lot of constant experimentation to where it is today.

If you are committed to starting a successful business or side hustle, you will achieve your goal if you keep experimenting and do not give up. You will find something that works for you. It might take you more or less time for you than it did for me, but it will happen if you do not give up., but it will happen if you do not give up. You only need to get it right once to end up with a successful venture and all the perks that come with being a successful business owner.

Stay inspired, keep experimenting, and do not give up.

CHAPTER 4: DEVELOPING RELATIONSHIPS

You have probably heard the phrase "It's not what you know, it's who you know" when talking about achieving success. The growth of my web design company and business network is undoubtedly a testament to this adage. However, the benefits of relationship building extend far beyond entrepreneurial and business endeavors. Successful relationship building can lead to job offers, promotions, and even long lasting personal relationships. It is vital to emphasize relationship building in your life and career.

Even if you do not believe you are in business development or sales, the reality is that you are. Relationships drive everything in the world around us, and you are selling at every stage of your life. We need to convince a college or program to accept our applications. We need to convince someone to go on a date with us. We need to convince our employers to hire us or give us a promotion. Without realizing it, we have to sell and build successful relationships at every point of our lives.

I was fascinated by accomplished entrepreneurs and innovators from a young age, and I desired to meet and network with influential people. When I was in the eighth grade, I created my LinkedIn profile and started connecting with people that summer. I worked on developing and optimizing my profile, and connecting with entrepreneurs and other people I could look up to. I looked at their resumes and researched their stories. At this point, I had no idea how I would develop relationships with these professionals.

Fast forward to today, I have developed and maintained relationships with several notably successful business clients throughout the country. In addition to the business clients I have attained, I have networked with and maintained relationships with prominent government officials like state representatives and U.S. representatives. I have been able to meet influential CEOs, Governors, Senators, public figures, White House Chiefs and Staff, two children of a former U.S. President, and the Vice President of the United States, all by the age of twenty-one. While getting to this point, I have gained invaluable insight into relationship building and networking. This chapter is divided into my five pieces of advice for building successful relationships and meeting successful people in your field.

First, realize your existing network. Many people do not realize the network they already have.

Whether it is school, a community activity, or another opportunity where you get to meet people, you already have a network. You already know people that can help you achieve your goals or introduce you to people that can help you achieve your goals.

When I was in my senior year of high school, wanting to start a digital consulting business, I did not know any local business owners and or how to connect with them. However, I found out that a classmate's dad started and owned a successful apparel manufacturing company in Hanover, PA. Since I was interested in creating a social media marketing agency, I messaged the Chief Executive Officer of the company, introduced myself, and asked to arrange a meeting with him. To increase the chances of the CEO opening my message, I also asked my classmate to pass along the message to his father. A day or two later, the CEO replied, and I was able to present my marketing ideas to him and other key company executives. Fortunately, his company became my first social media consulting client.

The following summer, my goal was to expand my services to include web design and development. One of my first web design clients was a local attorney and photographer. Though I did not know him personally, his brand was all over social media as a sports and portrait photographer for local high school students So, I went on his law firm website and saw that it was outdated, and he was definitely in need of web design services. I sent the attorney a message on social media, introduced myself as a recent graduate of South Western High School, and offered to take him out to lunch to talk about his website.

Fortunately, he agreed, and I arranged a meeting with him. During our lunch, we introduced ourselves thoroughly and started talking about his website. He was hesitant to choose a recent high school graduate to develop the new website for his law firm. Prepared for this hesitation, I prepared a demo with a home page for his review. I pulled up the mobile website demo, during our lunch, for him to view. However, he was not entirely sold by the end of our lunch and said he needed time to think.

I told him I understood and that he should reach out to me with any questions or concerns. I followed up via text message to thank him for his time and remind him to reach out to me with any questions or concerns. A few days later, after reviewing the desktop site demo, he agreed to hire me to develop his website. I ended up designing and maintaining the websites for his law firm and his photography business.

Another businessman that became a web design client was someone that I talked to at the gym. We were catching up one day, and I brought up that I started a web design company and told him about some of the clients I was working with. Interestingly enough, he was interested in starting a commercial cleaning company with his mother. He had already hired a firm in Maryland to develop his website, but he still wanted to talk to me. So, we decided to meet at Starbucks, and I reviewed his site that this other firm was building for him. I pointed out what I would have done differently, and helped him with a few digital tasks on the spot, like sourcing stock images for his website. Impressed with my insight, he said that he would follow up and keep me up to date. A few days later, he sent me a text message saying that he was unhappy with the work this firm was doing, and even though he already paid this firm, he wanted me to design the website for his business.

These first clients remind me not to forget the people that are already in my network. Most of the time, all you have to do is connect with them to develop the relationship further and tell them about what you want to do. When the relationship is strong enough, your connection will likely help you in whatever you are trying to achieve.

Second, expand your network to maximize your chances of doing business with people or taking on new opportunities. While official networking groups and events do exist, I do not go to these events. I started meeting potential clients at events and conferences where I did not intend to make business deals. It is more effective if you seek to meet like-minded people and pursue relationships with them rather than see it as a networking opportunity for you to get clients. All of us have our interests and hobbies, and there are plenty of events or conferences related to these interests.

As for me, I was always interested in making an impact on the public policy process. I looked for events and opportunities online and applied for them. In the summer of 2019, I attended a three-day political activism workshop in Arlington, VA. (outside of Washington D.C.), without any intent on pitching my web design business or acquiring new clients. One of the speakers who came on to do a presentation was a digital consultant with his own firm. Initially surprised by this, it eventually made sense. I realized the immense business opportunity that was right in front of me. Luckily, I brought my business cards and aimed to pass them out and tell people about my web design company. I talked to several congressional candidates, told them what I could offer them, and answered any questions relating to the digital side of political campaigns. Because we attended this three-day workshop together, they were easy clients to sell. Besides the speaker, who was only there briefly, I was the only person offering them web design services, and we had an existing bond because of our like-mindedness. After the workshop, I kept in touch and followed up on three promising leads.

Successfully, all three of the leads ended up being long-term clients of Patel Digital LLC. These clients were from Virginia, Tennessee, and Florida. My business partner at the time and I got to fly to Nashville and West Palm Beach that summer to work on big projects for these clients.

Since finding clients at this workshop was a tremendous success, I wanted to replicate this to find more clients; so I started attending other political conferences. Many clients and connections were successfully acquired at these conferences. Though you might think most of these clients would be political candidates or organizations, they were largely business owners.

Many business owners are highly invested in the advocacy of their industry and small businesses. The presence of business owners at these events makes for a tremendous opportunity to network and find clients.

Initially wanting to contribute to candidates whose policy positions I supported, I realized it was another tremendous opportunity to get clients. Through conferences and keeping up with politics, I found various fundraisers for candidates. To attend most fundraisers, you have to donate a minimum of $250, with many donors contributing more. Hence, most of the attendees of these fundraisers are either prolific business owners or are well connected to prolific business owners.

In 2020, I flew down to Orlando, Florida to attend a fundraiser for a young congressional candidate I supported. During this fundraiser, I introduced myself and my company to many attendees. After the fundraiser, I connected with a few individuals on social media and sent them text messages to have further conversations.

Months later, I attended another conference in Orlando. Before the conference, I messaged two individuals from the fundraiser to set up informal meetings with them. One of these individuals was a fanatstic connector who was able to invite me to a private event, where I met public figures and networked with other potential clients. Another gentleman from the fundraiser happened to be a healthcare entrepreneur that owned multiple pharmacies throughout Florida. Patel Digital has completed multiple web design projects for this individual. Rather than attending random networking events, I found that connecting with new people with similar interests and a similar mindset results in stronger relationships. These strong relationships then lead to business and career opportunities.

Third, it is fundamental to realize that you will not meet the most influential people in your field overnight. Like almost everything in business and in life, you have to remain consistent and trust the process. I was not able to shake the hand of the Vice President when I first started developing relationships.

There is a snowball effect, but it starts small. The story of how I started learning about many of these political conferences is interesting to reflect on. When I was a senior in high school, a college student became a newly elected school board member. This was interesting to me since it was a first for our high school. Since we shared similar political beliefs, I decided to reach out to him during my freshman year of college. I was also very interested in how he became the youngest member of the school board while still in college. We ended up meeting for coffee and conversation.A few months later, he told me about a political conference happening in Philadelphia that I should attend. He connected me with people from my college who were going to the conference, and I ended up registering. This conference in Philadelphia is also where I found out about the workshop that helped me attain three of my clients. The following fall, I ended up attending more conference and eventually ended up meeting up with my favorite U.S. Senator in Detroit, Michigan. Without this initial coffee meeting, so many connections would not have happened. If you start small and stay consistent, you will get to where you want to be.

Fourth, your mindset when approaching relationships is critical. Many people have a weak approach to building relationships. The focus should not be on the money or even getting a customer for your service; you should have a genuine interest in developing strong relationships with like-minded people. Selling a client is a byproduct of successful networking.

When I meet with people, I am genuinely interested in getting to know them and their stories. I want to see how I can add value to their life, which can be in a multitude of ways. Obviously, I can help web design clients with their websites. But there are so many other ways I can add value to someone. For example, I might introduce them to someone in my network and help them with lead generation. I could also donate to someone's cause or provide insight on something else that I may be knowledgeable about.

Ultimately, like any consumer, business

owners pay to have problems solved. Similarly, public figures like politicians will surround themselves with people who add value to them. If you want to have elected officials in your network, it is not that hard. You just have to show some sort of value to them. Your importance to politicians does not even have to be a monetary contribution. It can be providing a service to their campaign, knocking on doors, or even making phone calls from your house. We act like the concept of karma is a weird phenomenon, but it seems like common sense once we think about it. If you do good things for others, you will be able to reap the rewards. The more people you develop positive relationships with, the more likely that you will get another business or career opportunity.

Lastly, it is crucial to maintain and sustain all the positive relationships that you build. You never know how a relationship will benefit your personal or professional life in the future, so you should make an effort to maintain it. Your relationship is not over once you complete a project for someone or after they help you with something. Social media and technology make it easy to keep in touch with people. Ask people about their lives or for career updates. You can even meet up for a meal or drink if you happen to be in the same city. After putting in all the effort to develop these strong relationships, it makes sense to make an effort to sustain them.

During the COVID-19 pandemic, I did not know how I would get new client projects without meeting people in person. Thankfully, that year was my best year. I was still able to get clients because of the relationships that I had maintained. There was a county commissioner I met in 2019. I connected with him at a York County event. He was the youngest county commissioner elected, and he seemed to be a successful networker. Having no intention of selling him anything, I genuinely connected with him and asked him about his career and future goals. Over a year later, I saw on his Facebook that he was starting a business consulting firm. I immediately reached out to him to talk about his digital presence. He is currently a valuable client, and I would not have found out about his career move if I had not maintained this relationship.

Another client is an attorney I connected with at a conference in Washington, D.C. Initially, this lawyer was actually not interested in a website, but agreed to meet with me anyway. I found out about this attorney since his law firm was contracted by a client of mine in West Palm Beach, Florida. I saw an interesting case he was working on and saw that his website could be drastically improved. I sent him a message on Facebook, and we agreed to meet at a conference in D.C. After we met, I addressed some of his concerns with outsourcing web design to a company like mine. He agreed to hear me out and asked for an outline of things I would change. Instead of an outline, I sent him a demo, and he soon drafted up a contract for the service agreement. However, our relationship did not stop there. Because I put in extra effort to maintain our personal and professional relationship, he has given countless referrals for my web design company at no cost to me. He has introduced me to numerous executives, candidates, political action committees, and organizations.

Because I was able to leverage existing connections, relationships, and referrals, I successfully ran my business during the pandemic. Ultimately, strong relationships are the best asset your business and life can have.

How can you add value to the people around you?

CHAPTER 5: CONTINUOUS INNOVATION

Innovation is not only important to the creation of a business, but it is vital for its continued success as well. An impressive business empire in my hometown of Hanover, Pennsylvania that I always admired is owned and run by a family of real estate moguls named the Burkentines. Burkentines Builders is in the business of real estate and have become a "one stop shop" for real estate consumers. The three Burkentines brothers who run the day-to-day operations of the company all graduated with engineering degrees and are responsible for leadership roles within the company. These individuals are Mike, Bryce, and Brian Burkentine.

Today, their company owns approximately one thousand rental units which equates to $300 million AUM (assets under management). Like any successful company, their business had to start somewhere. The story of the Burkentines began in 1989.

Their father, Paul Burkentine, started the company in 1989. He started by building a duplex, a multi-family home that has two units in one building, while still employed with the National Security Agency. Paul and his wife continued to develop these duplexes until he finally quit the NSA to focus on growing a real estate business.

Since then, their company has also transitioned into land development, rental properties, and property management. Unlike many of their competitors, they can serve their consumers throughout every step of the real estate process. Expanding to be able to do this is called vertical integration, where a company expands into additional products and services that are in the same business but in different stages of production or distribution. Burkentine Builders employs about one hundred and thirty employees with about thirty of those involved in managerial roles.

This kind of growth was only able to be achieved by a lot of hard work and innovation. One of the key pivotal moments of Burkentine Builders happened during the recession of 2008 and 2009. While we may not have been personally affected, we have all heard and learned about the detrimental effects of the economic collapse during that time. While many companies in real estate and other industries were failing, Paul Burkentine used this hurdle to become stronger and eventually saw an opportunity to transition their company into the rental market.

Bryce Burkentine credits this pivotal point to both creating the successful mogul that their father became as well as the company they have today. Bryce says that "If you are not innovating every day, you are failing." He is an avid believer in always challenging the status quo.

Like many innovative companies, they rely on customer feedback to make managerial decisions within their company. If the main objective of your business and brand is to create relationships, it is fundamental to understand what your consumer needs. Also, their needs are always changing. Burkentine Builders gets this consumer feedback in a lot of ways. Because of their commitment to maintaining and developing a digital presence, they can get direct feedback from consumers and potential consumers about what their needs are.

In addition to their digital feedback, they rely on market surveys and conduct research on existing and predictive trends on the real estate market. With a constantly evolving economy, demand is always shifting based on a variety of factors. By understanding how economic changes affect their industry and receiving direct feedback from consumers, they can better service the needs of their consumers.

There are many innovative initiatives they have executed from this feedback. They continue to strive to be a leader in the rental market because of a generational shift towards wanting more travel flexibility. They predict that consumers will be more likely to rent a home rather than own it because of an increase in moving jobs and traveling more frequently.

In addition to a trend in home ownership, there

is also an obvious trend in electric car ownership versus traditional gasoline powered cars. Because of this trend, they are beginning to have charging stations on their rental properties.

Another trend they noticed as an effect of the pandemic is the demand for having work offices and amenities at home. Even after the pandemic, they predict that consumers will want these work amenities because of some aspects of work staying remote. Burkentine Builders is building their new properties with these consumer needs in mind.

Innovation starts within the company and Burkentine Builders strives to ensure their employees and goals reflect that. They use a value orientated approach in their hiring process to ensure the employees they hire will reflect their mission. They integrate their employees with digital collaboration tools that allow them to work efficiently, and their management team is all in one building allowing them to have that face-to-face interaction for important communication.

In five to ten years, they hope to reach $1 billion AUM (assets under management) which is about five thousand rental units leading to $400-500 million in revenue each year. Currently, they are at about one thousand rental units and have $300M AUM. With their commitment to continous innovation, it makes reaching these high goals possible.

How are you continuously innovating in your career and life?

CHAPTER 6:
MODERN MONEY

Money affects almost every aspect of our lives, yet most high school and college students do not seem to know much about personal finance. Because personal finance is a subject I frequently read about and studied, I knew of its importance. I also began to notice how most of my peers had little to no knowledge of the subject.

In high school, I served on an advisory committee with students from all grade levels who gave the administrators our perspective on various issues regarding the school. One of the things I heavily advocated for was a personal finance course that would empower students to take their financial future into their own hands.

A personal finance course eventually became a requirement to graduate, which was a significant step in the right direction. However, it is still not sufficient financial education. Because of a constantly evolving digital landscape, confusion and misconceptions surrounding financial topics only continue to worsen. While you should consult a certified financial advisor on specific investing matters, I hope to introduce you to some key financial concepts.

First and foremost, many people do not know the importance of investing. They do not think it is necessary, and they follow the old advice that only tells them to save their money. While saving money is incredibly important, investing allows you to grow your wealth and build for your retirement. It is something that everyone should do regardless of how much income they have.

You might wonder what is wrong with a traditional savings account. While interest rates were high at points in our history, today, they almost make no impact. Most banks give 0.02% or 0.01% interest which will not significantly impact most savings accounts. You are losing the value of your money by only using savings accounts and not utilizing other investment vehicles.

You are losing the value of your money because of an economic concept called inflation. All of us are affected by inflation, even if we do not realize it. When we shop for the same items like milk and eggs, but they gradually increase in price year to year, we are experiencing inflation. The consumer price index or CPI is the economic indicator that measures inflation. According to the United States Department of Labor Bureau of Labor Statistics, the CPI represents changes in prices of all goods and services purchased for consumption by urban households.

On average, the consumer price index is 2%, meaning that the cash sitting in your savings account is losing value at that rate every year. To offset the effects of inflation, you have to grow your assets by at least 2% every year. An ordinary savings account will not achieve this for you. Therefore, you need to explore other investment vehicles to get a head start on building your wealth.

Second, people do not realize the compound effect and the importance of starting early. Because investments like the stock market and high-yield savings accounts earn compound interest, you earn gains on your gains. When you get a chance, look up a graph depicting compound interest compared to a graph of simple interest. Essentially, simple interest has linear results, while a curve represents compound interest.

The more you wait and the earlier you start, the curve gets steeper. Therefore, you should capitalize on the time you have and start investing in your future as soon as you can.

Third, many people can not recognize the difference between investing and gambling. Because of social media and constant exposure to current events, we constantly hear about investments like cryptocurrency and NFTs (non-fungible tokens). Like all business endeavors, you should not make a significant investment in an industry you are not well educated in. If you invest in a cryptocurrency just because your friends or some influencer is telling you to, you are not investing. Allocating your money like this is no different than playing in a casino in Las Vegas.

Fourth, people think they need to invest a lot of time to have a diverse portfolio. However, you can participate in the stock market without spending much time deciding on specific companies. The S&P 500 index (Standard and Poor 500 Index) is an index that tracks the top 500 public companies in the United States. Investing in an ETF (exchange-traded fund) that tracks the S&P 500 like Vanguard's ETF (ticker symbol of$VOO) allows you to invest in this index and receive instant diversification.

Investing in an S&P 500 ETF can be an exceptional tool to start growing your wealth. According to Investopedia, the S&P 500 has grown approximately 10% in terms of average annual gain. Of course, there are years when there is a loss, but this has been a time-tested investment vehicle over time. In fact, during the 2020 Berkshire Hathaway shareholder's meeting, Warren Buffett claimed that "for most people, the best thing to do is to own the S&P 500 index fund."

Lastly, even some young people do not realize how easily they can open a brokerage account and make their first investments. Because of digital technology, you can setup an individual brokerage account on TD Ameritrade or Charles Schwab and start investing for your future today. You can view or make changes to your investment portfolio directly from your smartphone.

What steps are you going to take to secure

your financial future?

CHAPTER 7: SERVANT LEADERSHIP

The idea of leadership has always been of interest to me. There are countless articles, training programs, and books on the subject. As I grew older, I continued to observe examples of leadership and ask successful leaders, from a variety of fields, what leadership meant to them.

A defining moment of learning about leadership, for me personally, surprisingly happened on a swim team during my high school years. I was seeking a nomination to the United States Military Academy at West Point during this time. Survival swimming is a required course that all cadets must take to complete the USMA curriculum. Unfortunately, I was not a proficient swimmer at the time, and I even feared the swimming requirements the military had after viewing the requirements.

Even though I knew there would be physical and mental challenges in pursuing this endeavor, I did not dismiss it because I knew the military could teach me a lot about leadership and make me a better person overall. So, I got out of my comfort zone and decided to join a swim team. I told my coaches my intent when joining the team, and they were excited to go on the journey with me.

When I first joined the team, I had no idea what I was doing. Despite that, I kept working hard and learned how to improve. I watched videos at home and seeked constant feedback and guidance from my coaches. I came in before practice and did extra laps after practice, which drastically improved my skills.

Months after the season was over, I focused on my application for the congressional nomination process. Randomly, I received a text message from my coach saying that I would be receiving an award at the banquet. Amused by this message, I asked why I would be the person to receive the award. I was certainly not the most talented swimmer on the team. My coach told me I was receiving a leadership award for the impact I had made on my teammates. I told him I was not sure what kind of impact I made.

Still confused about how I made the most impact as a leader, I dressed up and showed up to the awards banquet. My coach got up on the stage and I knew it was coming, so I started to laugh to myself and remained curious about what he was going to say. He called me up to the front of the room, and he started speaking. He talked about how my teammates observed how determined I was to become better and inspired them to work harder. He said my teammates told him they wanted to work harder because of me.

Not realizing this at the time, I learned indispensable leadership lessons from this experience. First, I realized the importance of taking risks and stepping out of my comfort zone, which is a theme that is represented throughout multiple chapters of this book. However, it is not only important in starting and growing a business but is also crucial in leading others in many areas such as sports teams, philanthropic activities, political causes, and any other type of organization. To grow as a leader, you need to show courage and not fear stepping out of your comfort zone. We all have areas that we can improve in but we need to embrace our challenges and realize how we can learn, grow and improve.

Second, this experience became the perfect anecdote for "actions speak louder than words." While I always had the personality to encourage and motivate others to achieve academic and professional success, my focus was not motivating my teammates on the swim team. It was my first time swimming competitively, and I was laser-focused on the military academy congressional nomination process. In spite of my personal intent, I still managed to inspire my teammates to work harder. All I did was focus on putting in genuine hard work to grow myself and maintain a positive attitude throughout the process. Even though I was not the best and had a lot of progress to be made when I started, I embraced the challenge and enjoyed the progress I was making. In addition, my coaches and teammates saw me being the first one in the pool, and the last one out. So, while I was not verbally encouraging anyone to do anything, my actions spoke for me and inspired others to work harder.

Lastly, I learned that being a true leader is not dependent on a title. Many people think they must have a title to be a leader. This experience showed me that this is not true at all. I did not have any leadership title or role at the time, yet I was able to inspire others to work harder and achieve better results for the team. Regardless of what type of organization or team you are a part of, you can start being a leader today. You do not need a title to put in the work, maintain a positive attitude or put yourself out of your comfort zone. Your peers will notice these changes, which will only lead to better results for your team or organization.

That same year, I received a congressional nomination from Congressman Scott Perry to the United States Military Academy. This accomplishment was a surreal moment as it culminated in all the academic, fitness and leadership efforts I put into this endeavor. While I did not ultimately attend West Point, I am incredibly grateful for this experience because it helped me grow as a person in almost every area.

One of the requirements of even applying for a congressional or senate nomination to attend a military academy is to sit in a panel interview. These panels consist of former military officers, entrepreneurs, academic leaders, and politicians. I thoroughly enjoyed my conversations with these panelists. I received many words of encouragement and advice as I was deciding on a new chapter in my life. One of the things I remember to this day is a former military officer telling me that if I can show my subordinates or peers that I have integrity and want the best thing for them, they will likely follow my lead. This was an interesting statement that I think about to this day.

Although I did not attend West Point, I completed a year of Army ROTC at Penn State University. My desire to do this was to push myself and develop the qualities that would make me a better leader. I could not think of a better opportunity for these two things than the ROTC program at my university. Ultimately, the military is a leadership development program more than anything else. During this experience, I certainly was pushed physically and mentally in many ways, and we were constantly reminded of the importance of leadership through the principles of loyalty, duty, respect, selfless service, honesty, integrity, and personal courage, acronym for LDRSHIP.

While seeking multiple leadership experiences for my resume during high school, I was selected to go on the NRECA Youth Tour to Washington, D.C. where we toured important monuments and buildings to our country's history, heard from speakers, and even discussed public policy issues with our elected representatives and senators. While at the 9/11 Pentagon Memorial, an Army major general (two-star general) spoke to our group. At the time, Major General David Wilmot was working at the Pentagon as the Director of the Joint Surgeon, National Guard. He was responsible for the medical readiness and advising the Army on healthcare issues relating to soldiers, airmen, inter-service matters, and issues of national security. Because of my interest in military medicine at the time, I talked with him one-on-one after he finished speaking to our group. I later connected with General Wilmot on LinkedIn and sent him a message reminding him how we had met. Years later, I reconnected with him to get his perspective on leadership for this chapter.

General David Wilmot joined the Army during his second year of medical school, through a medical officer training corps partnership with his medical school. He served an incredible 31 years in the U.S. Army. Because of his experience and insight from various fields, I asked what he learned about leadership from each of his experiences. Then, I proceeded to ask him about his military experience. He talked about how the military has very formal leadership training. It develops in your military career as you transition from tactical leadership in completing objectives or missions, operational leadership in organizing and managing change and eventually strategic leadership in dealing with national security matters.

First, he mentioned the importance of mentorship with regards to leadership. He talked about how important it was to seek mentors and their guidance early on. Then, after you progress into senior roles, it is also your responsibility to give back by mentoring others. Next, he talked about the importance of honest and open communication and how people can sense when you are not genuine.

After asking him about his leadership insights from the military, I asked him about his lessons about leadership from medicine. He talked about how there were different levels of leadership in medicine because leading your staff and partners is going to be different from being a leader for your patient communities.

General Wilmot discussed how the medical community looks for your expertise and competency when dealing with staff and partners. While you must appear competent in your duties, this also means admitting when you do not know something. When leaders do not understand something, they ask questions and do research instead of acting like they know everything. For this medical example, referring to appropriate specialists when a medical issue is out of one's scope of practice is the appropriate action. It is also essential to keep learning because of constant change happening in the field.

When dealing with patients, it is imperative to listen and be empathic. Physicians consistently see patients that are dealing with healthcare issues that are significantly affecting their lives. Often, the doctor has no idea what it is like to have the disease or illness in question. Therefore, it is necessary to show empathy and to listen to the patient. This empathy aspect of leadership in medicine is applicable to leadership in any environment.

After talking to General Wilmot about the leadership lessons he learned from his military and medical experiences, I asked him about his business experiences after his military career and about what he is currently doing. General Wilmot is presently the Chief Medical Officer (CMO) of LTS Inc., a technology company in Washington D.C. that is involved in healthcare operations. Currently, he is working on turnkey COVID-19 vaccination programs across the United States and working on getting the vaccine to underserved urban and rural communities.

To accomplish this ambitious goal, they partner with Historically Black Colleges and Universities (HBCUs) and faith-based organizations to get the message out. Their company provides the materials, staff, and logistical support. At the same time, the HBCUs and faith-based organizations manage the public health communication regarding the vaccine. This way, the concerned citizens of various communities are not receiving communication from sources they might be skeptical of; they receive it from sources they trust and are accustomed to.

To wrap up my conversation with General Wilmot about leadership, I asked him how we should solve leadership challenges that are inevitably going to arise. First, we discussed how leadership challenges could be difficult to handle because they deal with people; the most complex type of asset in any organization. He talked about disciplinary actions when a mission or business objective fails and how it is challenging but crucial to take the appropriate action even if you are not a confrontational person. However, it does not stop here. To devise a solution to change human behavior and solve that leadership challenge, you must communicate clearly with the person. You need to ask them about their perspective on the issue at hand and if they agree or disagree with your assessment of the given situation.

General Wilmot went on to talk about how, in the military, they made this type of communication clear, which is not always done well in all private sector companies. Even from my personal experience in ROTC, anytime there would be a performance or disciplinary action, there would be a written account of the conversation so there could be no discrepency in the future. Also, leaders would create a plan of action and follow up. This type of problem solving can be effective for solving leadership challenges in any kind of organization or on any team.

Ultimately, leadership is an important skill to develop as we aim to grow in our lives and serve others.

CHAPTER 8:
PUBLISHING
POSSIBILITIES

The process of publishing this book itself is a case study of starting a new business venture. This process reinforced many of the principles that I discuss in previous chapters. While publishing a book was always one of my goals, I never expected to publish a book so soon.

When you think of starting a new business or publishing a book, it might seem intimidating and so far away from where you are. However, it is much closer than you think, and you are more than able to achieve the milestones you want.

After my friend and business partner Patrick Kane convinced me to publish my insights about entrepreneurship, I seriously considered the idea. About two months before submitting the first manuscript, I ran a poll on my Instagram story to ask my followers if I should publish a book on my entrepreneurial experience. I knew this was the best way to get initial feedback on whether this was an idea worth pursuing.

When I saw the results of this poll, 80% of the respondents had said yes, and I received many messages encouraging me to do so. Because I saw an apparent demand for a published version of my thoughts and experiences, I decided to research the publishing process. I discovered two publishing routes: getting a traditional publisher to publish my book or self-publishing.

Through my research on the internet and watching videos, I realized that self-publishing was the route I wanted to pursue various reasons. Most importantly, traditional publishers do not typically help authors with marketing anymore. My experience in digital marketing and web design would allow me to leverage those skills to market my book to consumers. Second, traditional publishers control the process, and you do not have the ultimate control throughout the process. Because I wanted to publish this book relatively quickly, I knew I could accomplish this through self-publishing.

After I had decided to pursue the self-publishing route, there were still countless decisions to be made. I needed to partner with a manufacturing and fulfillment company in the book printing space that would allow me to utilize a print-on-demand model. With a POD model, I only have to pay the manufacturing costs, or "costs of goods sold", after a consumer places an order on the website. Therefore, there are no overhead costs associated with this model. POD, or print-on-demand, business models allow entrepreneurs and creators to start many kinds of e-commerce ventures with little capital. I decided to partner with Amazon KDP to print and fulfill the order for my book.

Even though I had decided on my fulfillment partner, there were still crucial factors to be addressed. Throughout writing and editing the content for this book, I gradually worked on important publishing aspects of the book. The book cover was one of these things. People do quite literally judge a book by its cover, and I knew it was vital to the publishing process.

I heavily utilized my Instagram followers to get feedback on different book cover variations and A/B split test virtually every part of the book cover. A/B split testing means you test two different variations of a design or marketing strategy. Because of social media following, you can receive quality consumer feedback for free. Even if you have to utilize paid advertisements for larger sample size, the investment for this consumer feedback is insignificant compared to traditional market research. I used this strategy, and my followers essentially decided the title, colors, center graphic, and publishing imprint. I did not have to guess what consumers would have preferred because I could ask them directly.

Through internet research, A/B testing, and perserverance, publishing a book to consumers was within reach. Furthermore, I decided to launch Innovation Publishing LLC to not only secure legal and financial perks for my published book but to also create a brand and help other aspiring authors in the future.

What is stopping you from achieving a goal that you have?

ACKNOWLEDGE-MENTS

There needs to be a book just to thank all the individuals and organizations that have influenced the person that I am today. I am simply a result of everyone in my life and would not be here without all the people I have crossed paths with. First and foremost, my parents Prakash and Varsha Patel instilled in me the important values of hard work and ethics. They always let me pursue entrepreneurial endeavors, allowed me to travel the world and always supported my journey no matter how unordinary. My younger brother Krish always provides me support and is always reliable for a good laugh when we talk.

The execution of writing and publishing this book was not taken seriously until my friend Patrick Kane convinced me to seriously consider it. Patrick is also a business partner and helps me remain accountable in my growth as an entrepreneur and businessman. Noah Staub is another friend from Hanover who has provided nothing but support and encouragement on this journey.

My friend from middle school Bri Martin is a truly extraordinary individual who I have had the pleasure to know since fifth grade. Her optimistic nature is always inspiring and encouraging. She serves as a sister figure to me and is always there to help me in any facet of my life.

My former business partners from high school Sean Wolfe and Joshua Cuddy helped turned me into the entrepreneur I am today. I would not have success in my current ventures without the plethora of learning experiences that occurred in my first businesses.

My college roommates Dominick Vender, Colt Robb, Christopher Castiglia, Christopher Alderfer and Luke Shank truly make my undergraduate college experience worthwhile and are always there for me through any struggle or obstacle. I met Dominick Vender at Penn State's new student orientation and have been close friends with him since. Dominick's parents Dominick and Lisa Vender as well as his sister Adriana Vender have truly become like my family.

Justin Fisher is another extremely impactful figure in my undergraduate experience both personally and professionally. We help each other grow in various entrepreneurial endeavors and can always have the best time eating out or traveling.

I owe any accomplishments I have to the many people who have helped me throughout the process. I am forever grateful for these mentors. Paige Wingert, CEO of L2 Brands LLC, became my first consulting client who took a chance on a high school student and that initial paycheck me bootstrap my business' first business cards, legal documentation and website. Mark Riggs, CEO of Hanover Capital Management, emphasized the importance of sales and networking when I was still in high school. That conversation three years ago will continue to impact me in any entrepreneurial endeavor I pursue.

Coach Nathaniel Murren taught me to not be afraid of failure in and outside of the weight room. The impact of his training and instruction is priceless. Kathy Miserendino, also an editor for this book, was my FBLA advisor in high school continues to be there for me to provide business counsel to this day.

Even during the pandemic, various people have only further encouraged my growth as an entrepreneur and activist. Dan Backer, founder of Political.law PLLC, and Chris Reilly, President of Oriole Consulting LLC, have been some of the best clients to work with and grow my professional networks from. Victoria Berlandi, whom I met in Guatemala on a medical volunteer trip, has served as a great friend that I look up to and constantly seek advice from.

I interviewed many incredible individuals to write content for this book. Audrey Henson and College to Congress shared details about their incredible growth as a nonprofit organization. Jack and James Dumoulin, savvy entrepreneur brothers from Austin, Texas, reinforced critical concepts in this book about executing ideas and digital entrepreneurship. Bryce Burkentine from Burkentine Builders provided numerous examples of how their family business continuous to agressively innovative. General David Wilmot gave excellent advice about leadership from his well-rounded career.

All of my other incredible friends I did not mention specifically have given me nothing but encouragement in this endeavor and I could not have publised this book without them. All of my Instagram followers who participated in the A/B testing for parts of this book were an incredible help.

CHAPTER 1 NOTES

What does the American dream mean to me? How can I help preserve these values?

CHAPTER 2 NOTES

What does a successful lifestyle look like to me?
What do I want to spend my time doing?

CHAPTER 3 NOTES

How can I test an idea that I have with the skills and resources at my disposal?

CHAPTER 4 NOTES

How can I add value to the people around me? Who do I want to meet and how can I connect with them?

CHAPTER 5 NOTES

How can I further innovate in my career and life? How am I becoming the better version of myself in the various aspects of my life?

CHAPTER 6 NOTES

What steps am I going to take to secure my financial future? When and how am I going to make my first investment?

CHAPTER 7 NOTES

Who are my mentors and role models? How am I going to serve others?

CHAPTER 8 NOTES

What is stopping me from achieving a goal that I have? What steps can I take to get closer to achieving this goal?

Made in the USA
Las Vegas, NV
12 July 2021

26327028R00052